The Complete Plant Based Diet for Beginners

Easy, Delicious & Healthy Recipes to Reset Your Body and Live a Healthy Life

(21-Day Meal Plan to Kickstart Your Healthy Lifestyle)

Dr Merdy Bouk

Table of contents

Introduction

Whether you are already convinced that plant-based eating is the best way to go, or just plain curious about this increasingly popular diet, this book will guide you in understanding the what's, how's and why's of a plant-based diet.

From celebrity advocates to social media campaigns, it has been evident in recent years how plant-based diets are becoming not just another fad but a sustainable lifestyle change.

In the United States alone, an estimate of at least a third of consumers in 2018 are switching to more plant-based foods, Forbes reported.

Research has shown that science supports how changing to a low-fat, whole-food, plant-based diet is a very powerful and holistic approach to avoid or reverse chronic diseases, and help the environment at the same time.

Moreover, plant-based eating is not too restrictive nor is it difficult to follow. You will find an array of easy, affordable and inspirational ideas on how to include more plant-based foods into your diet—from main hearty meals and quick creative lunches to refreshing juices and smoothies and fun tasty desserts.

In contrast, most fad diets are very motivating at first but eventually fail because eliminating and restricting food groups may end up backfiring by increasing your risks of getting sick.

Still not sure if you can commit to eating plant-based foods100 percent? No need to worry. The following chapters will show you in detail how you do not need to approach a plant-based diet with an all-or-nothing attitude. Rest assured that every step you take is a step closer to lowered risks of developing chronic diseases, and higher energy levels through a plant-based diet that you can stick with for the rest of your longer and healthier life.

Chapter 1: Understanding the Plant Based Diet

What Is Plant Based Diet?

A plant-based diet is not synonymous to a vegetarian or vegan diet. Although these terms are often used interchangeably, they are not the same.

A plant-based diet is focused on proportionately eating more foods primarily from plants and cutting back on animal-derived foods. However, it does not necessarily involve eliminating entire food groups and lean sources of protein. This means, those on a plant-based diet may still opt to eat some meat.

Going vegan, on the other hand, means being strictly against animal products in any form—from never eating meat and dairy products to not patronizing products tested on animals and not wearing animal products such as leather.

A healthy plant-based diet generally emphasizes meeting your nutritional needs by eating more whole plant foods, while reducing the intake of animal products. Whole foods refer to natural, unrefined or minimally refined foods. Plant foods consist of those that do not have animal ingredients such as meat, eggs, honey, milk and other dairy products.

In contrast, those on a vegetarian diet may still eat processed and refined foods. Vegetarians can even eat fast foods, junk food and other salty snacks guilt-free.

Benefits of Plant Based Diet

There are many benefits that you can enjoy once you shift to a plant-based diet.

One is that it has been proven to help ward off many serious ailments, including but not limited to the following:

- Heart disease
- High blood pressure
- Hypertension
- Type 2 diabetes

- Certain forms of cancer

Not only that, it is also said to play a role in the prevention of degenerative medical conditions such as multiple sclerosis and Alzheimer's disease.

Once you get started with this diet, you will notice a huge difference in how you feel each day. From the time that you wake up in the morning, you will feel that you have more energy, and that you do not get tired as easily as before. You will also have more mental focus and fewer mood-related problems.

As for digestion, a plant-based diet is also said to improve how the digestive system works. In fact, dieters confirm fewer incidences of stomach pains, bloating, indigestion and hyperacidity.

Then there's the weight loss benefit that we cannot forget about. Since a plant-based diet means eating fruits, vegetables, and whole grains that have fewer calories and are lower in fat, you will enjoy weight loss benefits that some other fad diets are not able to provide.

Aside from helping you lose weight; it maintains ideal weight longer because this diet is easier to sustain and does not require elimination of certain food groups.

Don't worry about not getting enough nutrients from your food intake. This diet provides all the necessary nutrients including proteins, vitamins, minerals, carbohydrates, fats, and antioxidants. And again, that's because it does not eliminate any food group but only encourages you to focus more on plant-based food products.

How Do You Start A Plant Based Diet?

Unlike with other diet programs, with the plant-based diet, you don't have to worry too much about getting stared.

As you will find out for yourself, getting started is not that difficult because most likely, you are already eating most of what is required. There's a big chance that you will only need to make minimal changes in your diet.

Here are the steps on how to get started:

Step # 1 – Write down your current diet

Do not make any changes with your diet first. For the first week, record all the dishes and snacks that you eat throughout the day. This will show you what areas in your food habits are necessary to be changed, and which ones can be retained.

Step # 2 – Write down a menu based on this diet

Once you're done with recording the past week's diet, you can now create your diet for the second week. Take note that you don't have to completely overhaul your diet immediately as this will make the transition too drastic and might not provide positive results.

Start avoiding some of the foods and drinks that are not encouraged in a plant-based diet. You should also start adding more fruits and vegetables to dishes that you love. For example, if you are fond of eating oatmeal in the morning, it would be a great idea to start packing it with bananas, apples and mangoes. If you love snacking on yogurt, make it a point to stir in some blueberries or strawberries.

Step # 3 – Cut down on meat consumption

Do not completely avoid all types of meat. But you just have to reduce intake slowly but surely. For instance, instead of eating steak with mashed potatoes on the side for dinner, why don't you try sautéing green beans with a few strips of beef and serve it with mashed potatoes on the side. This way, there are more vegetables than meat in your dish.

Step # 4 – Fill your pantry with healthy items

It's a lot harder to adopt a healthy diet if you kitchen is filled with all sorts of junk foods. Discard the candies, sweet treats, sugary beverages and bags of chips that are in your pantry. Replace these with natural and healthy snacks like kale chips, whole grain bread slices, and fruit desserts.

What to Eat

Here's a list of all the foods and drinks that you should focus on while on a plant-based diet:

- Fruits – Apples, bananas, blueberries, blackberries, pears, oranges, mangoes, avocados, pineapple, strawberries, raspberries
- Vegetables – Spinach, tomatoes, carrots, cucumber, zucchini, potatoes, squash, broccoli, cauliflower, kale, cabbage
- Whole grains – Brown rice, quinoa, oats, barley, whole wheat bread, whole wheat pasta
- Legumes – Peanuts, beans, peas, chickpeas, lentils
- Plant-based protein – Tempeh, tofu
- Nuts – Almonds, walnuts, pistachios
- Nut butters
- Seeds – Sunflower seeds, flax seeds
- Healthy oils – Olive oil, avocado oil, grapeseed oil
- Herbs and spices
- Water
- Coffee
- Tea
- Smoothies
- Fresh fruit or veggie juices

Now, here's a list of all the foods and drinks that you can consume but try to limit intake as much as possible.

- Meat – Beef, pork, lamb
- Poultry – Chicken, turkey
- Seafood – Fish, shells, crabs, shrimp
- Dairy products – Milk, cheese, yogurt
- Processed meats - Bacon, sausage

What to Avoid

This one is a list of the foods and drinks that you would want to avoid as much as possible.

- Fast food

- Sweetened beverages
- Refined grains – White bread, white rice, refined pasta
- Packaged foods – Cookies, chips, cereals

Tips

Make the transition for you easier using the following tips and strategies:

- Make a meal planner

Write down a menu for the week or for the month so you don't have to worry about steering away from your healthy diet. It would be a good idea to make use of an online meal planner that you can access even when you're outside your home. But if you prefer to do it the traditional way, and write it on paper, that is a good idea too.

- Eat small healthy snacks during the day

Doing this will keep you full longer and will reduce the possibility of getting tempted to eat foods that are not encouraged in a plant-based diet. If you are full, there's less tendency for you to crave for a huge slab of steak for instance.

- Don't be too hard on yourself

Making a transition from one diet to another is always difficult and challenging. Do not expect yourself to be immediately comfortable with your new diet. It may take you longer than a week. It would probably require you at least a month to ease in to your new diet, even if this is not as restrictive as other types of diet.

- Use meat as garnish

Instead of making it the centerpiece of your dish, use it as an "add-on". Instead of serving steak with a small number of steamed veggies on the side, it would be better to turn things around and serve more steamed veggies and just a little amount of meat.

- Use good fats

Make it a point to use only healthy fats like olive oil, avocados, nut butter and so on.

- Have lots of salads

Salads are a great way to turn your regular diet into one that's plant-based. Not only that, these are extremely convenient to prepare and will only take you a few minutes to prepare. You won't have to spend a long time in the kitchen to cook an elaborate meal.

- Satisfy cravings for sweets with fruits

There will always be those times when you will crave for something sweet. For some people, this usually happens after a meal. Do not deprive yourself. Instead, satisfy your craving the healthy way—eat fruits for dessert.

Follow these tips to ensure to have a smooth transition from your old diet into this new one. It may not be as challenging as with other diet programs, but of course, there will also be certain drawbacks that you would want to be prepared for.

Chapter 2: 21-Day Meal plan

Day 1

Breakfast: Avocado and Egg Salad on Toasted Bread

Lunch: Turkey Sandwich

Dinner: Veggie Marinara

Day 2

Breakfast: Cottage Cheese, Honey and Raspberries

Lunch: Eggplant Parmesan

Dinner: Roasted Veggies

Day 3

Breakfast: Apple Pancakes

Lunch: Green Pizza with Bacon

Dinner: Korean Beef and Cabbage

Day 4

Breakfast: Arugula, Tomato and Olive Omelet

Lunch: Roasted Vegetables and Sausage Sandwich

Dinner: Grilled Zucchini with Tomato Salsa

Day 5

Breakfast: Scrambled Eggs with Spinach

Lunch: Broccoli Pasta with Turkey

Dinner: Green Beans with Bacon

Day 6

Breakfast: Avocado and Egg Salad on Toasted Bread

Lunch: Tofu with Collard Greens

Dinner: Baked Halibut with Brussels Sprouts

Day 7

Breakfast: Cottage Cheese, Honey and Raspberries

Lunch: Citrus Salad

Dinner: Potato and Artichoke Gratin

Day 8

Breakfast: Pineapple Bagel with Cream Cheese

Lunch: Red Bell Pepper Salad

Dinner: Veggie Marinara

Day 9

Breakfast: Waffles with Pumpkin & Cream Cheese

Lunch: Avocado Salad in a Sandwich

Dinner: Chickpea Dumplings

Day 10

Breakfast: Apple Pancakes

Lunch: Vegetable Wraps

Dinner: Tofu and Mushroom Stir-Fry

Day 11

Breakfast: Herb and Cheese Omelet

Lunch: Sweet Potato Hash with Kale

Dinner: Green Beans with Bacon

Day 12

Breakfast: Arugula, Tomato and Olive Omelet

Lunch: Roasted Veggies

Dinner: Zoodles with Avocado Pesto

Day 13

Breakfast: Scrambled Eggs with Spinach

Lunch: Baked Halibut with Brussels Sprouts

Dinner: Korean Beef and Cabbage

Day 14

Breakfast: Cream Cheese Waffles

Lunch: Red Bell Pepper Salad

Dinner: Chickpea Dumplings

Day 15

Breakfast: Cottage Cheese, Honey and Raspberries

Lunch: Spinach, Strawberry and Avocado Salad

Dinner: Zucchini Fritters

Day 16

Breakfast: Oatmeal Pancake

Lunch: Sweet & Sour Tofu with Peas

Dinner: Turkey Sandwich

Day 17

Breakfast: Waffles with Pumpkin & Cream Cheese

Lunch: Grilled Zucchini with Tomato Salsa

Dinner: Tofu with Collard Greens

Day 18

Breakfast: Pineapple Bagel with Cream Cheese

Lunch: Zoodles with Avocado Pesto

Dinner: Wine-Roasted Mushrooms

Day 19

Breakfast: Cream Cheese Waffles

Lunch: Roasted Vegetables and Sausage Sandwich

Dinner: Green Beans with Roasted Red Peppers

Day 20

Breakfast: Oatmeal Pancake

Lunch: Chopped Cucumber, Tomato and Radish Salad

Dinner: Eggplant Curry

Day 21

Breakfast: Herb and Cheese Omelet

Lunch: Baked Halibut with Brussels Sprouts

Dinner: Sweet and Sour Tofu with Peas

Chapter 3: Breakfast

Apple Pancakes

Preparation Time: 15 minutes
Cooking Time: 4 minutes
Servings: 4

Ingredients:

- 1 cup whole-wheat flour
- ¾ tsp. ground cinnamon, divided
- ¼ tsp. baking soda
- 1 tsp. baking powder
- Pinch salt
- 1 egg
- ¾ cup ricotta cheese
- 1 cup buttermilk
- 1 tsp. vanilla extract
- 1 tbsp. sugar and 1 tsp. sugar, divided
- 1 apple, sliced into rings
- 4 tsp. butter
- 4 tsp. walnut oil

Method:

1. In a bowl, mix the flour, ½ teaspoon cinnamon, baking soda, baking powder and salt.
2. In another bowl, beat the eggs and stir in the cheese, milk, vanilla and 1 tablespoon sugar.
3. Gradually add the second bowl to the first one. Mix well.
4. Combine the remaining cinnamon and 1 teaspoon sugar in a separate dish.
5. Coat each apple ring with this mixture.
6. Pour the butter and oil in a pan over medium heat.

7. Add the apples and pour the batter around the apple.
8. Cook for 2 minutes.
9. Flip and cook for another 2 minutes.

Nutritional Value:

- Calories 342
- Total Fat 16 g
- Saturated Fat 7 g
- Cholesterol 83 mg
- Sodium 448 mg
- Total Carbohydrate 38 g
- Dietary Fiber 4 g
- Protein 13 g
- Total Sugars 12 g
- Potassium 252 mg

Cream Cheese Waffles

Preparation Time: 5 minutes

Cooking Time: 0 minute

Serving: 1

Ingredients:

- 1 whole-grain waffle
- 1 tbsp. cream cheese
- 1 tbsp. granola
- 1 plum, sliced

Method:

1. Toast the waffle.
2. Place it on a plate.
3. Spread the top with cream cheese.
4. Arrange granola and plum, and serve.

Nutritional Value:

- Calories 188
- Total Fat 10 g
- Saturated Fat 4 g
- Cholesterol 15 mg
- Sodium 219 mg
- Total Carbohydrate 25 g
- Dietary Fiber 5 g
- Protein 4 g
- Total Sugars 10 g
- Potassium 225 mg

Herb & Cheese Omelet

Preparation Time: 5 minutes
Cooking Time: 5 minutes
Servings: 2

Ingredients:

- 4 eggs
- Salt and pepper to taste
- 2 tbsp. low-fat milk
- 1 tsp. chives, chopped
- 1 tbsp. parsley, chopped
- ½ cup goat cheese, crumbled
- 1 tsp. olive oil

Method:

1. Beat the eggs in a bowl.
2. Stir in the salt, pepper and milk.
3. In a bowl, combine the chives, parsley and goat cheese.
4. Pour the oil into a pan over medium heat.
5. Cook the eggs for 3 minutes.
6. Add the cheese mixture on top.
7. Fold and serve.

Nutritional Value:

- Calories 227
- Total Fat 17 g
- Saturated Fat 7 g
- Cholesterol 397 mg
- Sodium 386 mg
- Total Carbohydrate 3 g
- Dietary Fiber 1 g
- Protein 17 g
- Total Sugars 1 g
- Potassium 183 mg

Pineapple Bagel with Cream Cheese

Preparation Time: 10 minutes
Cooking Time: 3 minutes
Servings: 8

Ingredients:

- 8 pineapple slices
- 4 tsp. brown sugar
- 4 whole-wheat bagels, sliced in half and toasted
- 6 oz. cream cheese
- 3 tbsp. almonds, toasted and sliced

Method:

1. Preheat your broiler.
2. Line your baking pan with parchment paper.
3. Place the pineapple slices on the baking pan
4. Sprinkle each with the sugar.
5. Broil the pineapples for 3 minutes.
6. Spread the cream cheese on top of the bagels.
7. Sprinkle almonds on top.
8. Top each bagel with the pineapple slices.

Nutritional Value:

- Calories 157
- Total Fat 6 g
- Saturated Fat 3 g
- Cholesterol 16 mg
- Sodium 167 mg
- Total Carbohydrate 23 g
- Dietary Fiber 4 g
- Protein 6 g
- Total Sugars 10 g
- Potassium 110 mg

Scrambled Eggs with Spinach

Preparation Time: 5 minutes
Cooking Time: 4 minutes
Servings: 2

Ingredients:

- 2 tsp. olive oil
- 3 cups baby spinach
- 4 eggs, beaten
- Salt and pepper to taste
- 2 slices whole-wheat bread, toasted
- 1 cup raspberries, sliced

Method:

1. Pour the olive oil into a pan over medium heat.
2. Cook the spinach for 2 minutes.
3. Transfer to a plate.
4. Add the eggs to the pan.
5. Cook while stirring frequently for 2 minutes.
6. Add the spinach and season with salt and pepper.
7. Serve scrambled egg on top of the bread, and with raspberries.

Nutritional Value:

- Calories 296
- Total Fat 16 g
- Saturated Fat 4 g
- Cholesterol 372 mg
- Sodium 394 mg
- Total Carbohydrate 21 g
- Dietary Fiber 7 g
- Protein 18 g
- Total Sugars 5 g
- Potassium 293 mg

Oatmeal Pancake

Preparation Time: 10 minutes
Cooking Time: 30 minutes
Servings: 8

Ingredients:

- ½ cup blueberries
- 3 bananas, sliced
- 2 tsp. lemon juice
- ¼ cup maple syrup
- ¼ tsp. ground cinnamon
- 1 cup flour
- 2 tsp. baking powder
- ½ tsp. baking soda
- ½ cup rolled oats
- Salt to taste
- 1 egg, beaten
- 1 cup buttermilk
- 1 tsp. vanilla
- 1 tbsp. olive oil

Method:

1. Toss the blueberries and bananas in lemon juice, maple syrup and cinnamon. Set aside.
2. In a bowl, mix the flour, baking powder, baking soda, oats and salt.
3. In another bowl, combine the egg, milk and vanilla.
4. Slowly add the second bowl mixture into the first one. Mix well.
5. Pour the oil into a pan over medium heat.
6. Pour 4 tablespoons of the batter and cook for 2 minutes per side.
7. Repeat with the remaining batter.
8. Serve the pancakes with the fruits.

Nutritional Value:

- Calories 159
- Total Fat 3 g
- Saturated Fat 0 g
- Cholesterol 1 mg
- Sodium 246 mg
- Total Carbohydrate 31 g
- Dietary Fiber 2 g
- Protein 5 g
- Total Sugars 8 g
- Potassium 260 mg

Waffles with Pumpkin & Cream Cheese

Preparation Time: 5 minutes
Cooking Time: 0 minute
Serving: 1

Ingredients:

- 1 whole-wheat waffle
- ½ oz. cream cheese
- 1 tbsp. canned pumpkin puree
- 1 tsp. walnuts, toasted and chopped

Method:

1. Toast the waffle.
2. Mix the cream cheese and pumpkin.
3. Spread the mixture on top of the waffle.
4. Sprinkle the walnuts on top.

Nutritional Value:

- Calories 132
- Total Fat 7 g
- Saturated Fat 2 g
- Cholesterol 10 mg
- Sodium 203 mg
- Total Carbohydrate 14 g
- Dietary Fiber 4 g
- Protein 4 g
- Total Sugars 2 g
- Potassium 310 mg

Avocado & Egg Salad on Toasted Bread

Preparation Time: 5 minutes

Cooking Time: 0 minute

Servings: 2

Ingredients:

- ½ avocado
- 1 tsp. lemon juice
- 2 hard-boiled egg, chopped
- 2 tbsp. celery, chopped
- Salt to taste
- 1 tsp. hot sauce
- 2 slices whole-wheat bread, toasted

Method:

1. Mash the avocado in a bowl.
2. Stir in the lemon juice, egg, celery, salt and hot sauce.
3. Spread the mixture on top of the toasted bread.

Nutritional Value:

- Calories 230
- Total Fat 14 g
- Saturated Fat 3 g
- Cholesterol 186 mg
- Sodium 405 mg
- Total Carbohydrate 17 g
- Dietary Fiber 5 g
- Protein 11 g
- Total Sugars 2 g
- Potassium 400 mg

Cottage Cheese, Honey & Raspberries

Preparation Time: 10 minutes

Cooking Time: 0 minute

Servings: 4

Ingredients:

- 2 cups fresh raspberries
- 1 tsp. lemon zest
- 2 tbsp. honey
- 2 cups cottage cheese
- 2 tbsp. sunflower seeds, roasted

Method:

1. Add 1 cup raspberry in your food processor.
2. Pulse until pureed.
3. Transfer to a bowl and stir in the lemon zest and honey.
4. Divide the cottage cheese among 4 bowls.
5. Top each one with the raspberry mixture.

Nutritional Value:

- Calories 169
- Total Fat 4 g
- Saturated Fat 1 g
- Cholesterol 5 mg
- Sodium 476 mg
- Total Carbohydrate 20 g
- Dietary Fiber 4 g
- Protein 16 g
- Total Sugars 15 g
- Potassium 230 mg

Chapter 4: Soups and Salads

Butternut Squash Soup

Preparation Time: 15 minutes

Cooking Time: 25 minutes

Servings: 6

Ingredients:

- 2 tbsp. olive oil
- 1 cup onion, chopped
- 1 cup cilantro
- 1 ginger, sliced thinly
- 2 cups pears, chopped
- ½ tsp. ground coriander
- Salt to taste
- 2 ½ lb. butternut squash, cubed
- 1 tsp. lime zest
- 26 oz. coconut milk
- 1 tbsp. lime juice
- ½ cup plain yogurt

Method:

1. Pour the oil into a pan over medium heat.
2. Add the onion, cilantro, ginger, pears, coriander and salt.
3. Stir and cook for 5 minutes.
4. Transfer to a pressure cooker.
5. Stir in the squash and lime zest.
6. Pour in the coconut milk.
7. Cook on high for 20 minutes.
8. Release pressure naturally.
9. Stir in the lime juice.

10. Transfer to a blender.
11. Pulse until smooth.
12. Reheat and stir in yogurt before serving.

Nutritional Value:

- Calories 274
- Total Fat 14 g
- Saturated Fat 8 g
- Cholesterol 3 mg
- Sodium 438 mg
- Total Carbohydrate 36 g
- Dietary Fiber 6 g
- Protein 5 g
- Total Sugars 11 g
- Potassium 715 mg

Lemon & Strawberry Soup

Preparation Time: 4 hours and 10 minutes

Cooking Time: 0 minute

Servings: 4

Ingredients:

- 1 cup buttermilk
- 3 cups strawberries, sliced
- 1 tsp. lemon thyme
- 2 tsp. lemon zest
- 2 tbsp. honey

Method:

1. Blend the buttermilk and strawberries in your food processor.
2. Transfer this mixture to a bowl.
3. Add the thyme and lemon zest.
4. Chill in the refrigerator for 4 hours.
5. Strain the soup and stir in the honey.
6. Serve in bowls.

Nutritional Value:

- Calories 92
- Total Fat 1 g
- Saturated Fat 0 g
- Cholesterol 2 mg
- Sodium 66 mg
- Total Carbohydrate 20 g
- Dietary Fiber 2 g
- Protein 3 g
- Total Sugars 17 g
- Potassium 266 mg

Tomato Soup with Kale & White Beans

Preparation Time: 5 minutes

Cooking Time: 7 minutes

Servings: 4

Ingredients:

- 28 oz. tomato soup
- 1 tbsp. olive oil
- 3 cups kale, chopped
- 14 oz. cannellini beans, rinsed and drained
- 1 tsp. garlic, crushed and minced
- ¼ cup Parmesan cheese, grated

Method:

1. Pour the soup into a pan over medium heat.
2. Add the oil and cook the kale for 2 minutes.
3. Stir in the beans and garlic.
4. Simmer for 5 minutes.
5. Sprinkle with Parmesan cheese before serving.

Nutritional Value:

- Calories 200
- Total Fat 6 g
- Saturated Fat 1 g
- Cholesterol 4 mg
- Sodium 355 mg
- Total Carbohydrate 29 g
- Dietary Fiber 6 g
- Protein 9 g
- Total Sugars 1 g
- Potassium 257 mg

Yogurt Soup with Rice

Preparation Time: 15 minutes

Cooking Time: 48 minutes

Servings: 6

Ingredients:

- ½ cup brown rice, rinsed and drained
- 1 egg
- 4 cups yogurt
- 3 tbsp. rice flour
- 3 cups water
- ½ cup mint, chopped
- ½ cup cilantro, chopped
- ½ cup dill, chopped
- ½ cup parsley, chopped
- 2 cups arugula
- Salt to taste

Method:

1. Combine the rice, egg, yogurt and flour in a pot.
2. Put it over medium heat and cook for 1 minute, stirring frequently.
3. Pour in the water and increase heat to boil.
4. Reduce heat and simmer for 45 minutes.
5. Add the arugula, herbs and salt.
6. Cook for 2 minutes.
7. Add more water to adjust consistency.

Nutritional Value:

- Calories 186
- Total Fat 7 g
- Saturated Fat 4 g

- Cholesterol 52 mg
- Sodium 486 mg
- Total Carbohydrate 24 g
- Dietary Fiber 2 g
- Protein 9 g
- Total Sugars 8 g
- Potassium 365 mg

Zucchini Soup

Preparation Time: 5 minutes

Cooking Time: 15 minutes

Servings: 4

Ingredients:

- 3 cups chicken broth
- 1 tbsp. tarragon, chopped
- 3 zucchinis, sliced
- 3 oz. cheddar cheese
- Salt and pepper to taste

Method:

1. Pour the broth into a pot.
2. Stir in the tarragon and zucchini.
3. Bring to a boil and then simmer for 10 minutes.
4. Transfer to a blender and blend until smooth.
5. Put it back to the stove and stir in cheese.
6. Season with salt and pepper.

Nutritional Value:

- Calories 110
- Total Fat 5 g
- Saturated Fat 3 g
- Cholesterol 15 mg
- Sodium 757 mg
- Total Carbohydrate 7 g
- Dietary Fiber 2 g
- Protein 10 g
- Total Sugars 4 g
- Potassium 606 mg

Citrus Salad

Preparation Time: 10 minutes

Cooking Time: 0 minute

Servings: 8

Ingredients:

- 3 tbsp. freshly squeezed lemon juice
- 5 tbsp. olive oil
- 2 tsp. Dijon mustard
- 2 tbsp. honey
- 1 tbsp. shallot, minced
- 1 tbsp. fresh thyme, chopped
- Salt and pepper to taste
- 4 cups mixed salad greens
- 2 cups radicchio leaves, shredded
- 3 oranges, sliced
- 1 grapefruit, sliced
- ¼ cup pomegranate seeds

Method:

1. Combine lemon juice, oil, mustard, honey, shallot, thyme, salt and pepper in a glass jar with lid.
2. Arrange the salad greens and radicchio leaves in a salad bowl.
3. Top with the oranges and grapefruit slices.
4. Sprinkle top with the pomegranate seeds.
5. Serve with the dressing on the side.

Nutritional Value:

- Calories 144
- Total Fat 9 g
- Saturated Fat 1 g

- Cholesterol 0 mg
- Sodium 167 mg
- Total Carbohydrate 16 g
- Dietary Fiber 2 g
- Protein 1 g
- Total Sugars 12 g
- Potassium 195 mg

Red Bell Pepper Salad

Preparation Time: 10 minutes
Cooking Time: 10 minutes
Servings: 4

Ingredients:

- 4 red bell peppers, sliced into quarters
- 4 oz. mozzarella cheese
- 3 tbsp. basil, chopped
- 1 tbsp. balsamic glaze
- 1 ½ tbsp. olive oil
- Salt and pepper to taste

Method:

1. Preheat your broiler.
2. Broil the bell peppers for 10 minutes.
3. Toss with the mozzarella and basil.
4. Drizzle with the balsamic glaze and olive oil.
5. Season with salt and pepper.

Nutritional Value:

- Calories 166
- Total Fat 13 g
- Saturated Fat 5 g
- Cholesterol 7 mg
- Sodium 307 mg
- Total Carbohydrate 9 g
- Dietary Fiber 1 g
- Protein 6 g
- Total Sugars 5 g
- Potassium 259 mg

Spinach Salad

Preparation Time: 10 minutes

Cooking Time: 0 minutes

Servings: 4

Ingredients:

- 2 tbsp. olive oil
- Salt and pepper to taste
- 4 tsp. vinegar
- 8 cups baby spinach
- 1 cup raspberries
- ¼ cup goat cheese, crumbled
- ¼ cup hazelnuts, toasted and chopped

Method:

1. Combine the vinegar, salt, pepper and oil in a bowl.
2. Toss the spinach and raspberries in this mixture.
3. Top with the goat cheese and hazelnuts.

Nutritional Value:

- Calories 172
- Total Fat 13 g
- Saturated Fat 2 g
- Cholesterol 3 mg
- Sodium 267 mg
- Total Carbohydrate 9 g
- Dietary Fiber 5 g
- Protein 5 g
- Total Sugars 2 g
- Potassium 434 mg

Chopped Cucumber, Tomato & Radish Salad

Preparation Time: 15 minutes
Cooking Time: 0 minute
Servings: 6

Ingredients:

- 1 tbsp. lemon juice
- ½ cup feta cheese, crumbled
- ½ cup mayonnaise
- Salt and pepper to taste
- 1 tbsp. fresh dill, chopped
- 1 tbsp. fresh chives, chopped
- 1 cucumber, diced
- 3 cups cherry tomatoes, chopped
- 2 cups radish, diced
- 1 onion, minced

Method:

1. Mix the lemon juice, feta cheese, mayo, salt, pepper, dill and chives in a bowl.
2. Stir in the rest of the ingredients.
3. Toss to coat evenly.

Nutritional Value:

- Calories 187
- Total Fat 17 g
- Saturated Fat 4 g
- Cholesterol 0 mg
- Sodium 40 mg
- Total Carbohydrate 9 g
- Dietary Fiber 2 g
- Protein 10 g
- Total Sugars 1 g
- Potassium 164 mg

Spinach, Strawberry & Avocado Salad

Preparation Time: 5 minutes
Cooking Time: 0 minute
Servings: 2

Ingredients:

- 6 cups baby spinach
- 1 cup strawberries, sliced
- 2 tbsp. onion, chopped
- ½ avocado, diced
- 4 tbsp. vinaigrette
- 4 tbsp. walnuts, toasted

Method:

1. Toss the spinach, strawberries, onion and avocado in the vinaigrette.
2. Sprinkle with the walnuts.

Nutritional Value:

- Calories 296
- Total Fat 18 g
- Saturated Fat 2 g
- Cholesterol 0 mg
- Sodium 195 mg
- Total Carbohydrate 27 g
- Dietary Fiber 10 g
- Protein 8 g
- Total Sugars 11 g
- Potassium 195 mg

Chapter 5: Main Dishes

Zoodles with avocado Pesto

Preparation Time: 45 minutes

Cooking Time: 5 minutes

Servings: 4

Ingredients:

- 6 zucchinis, sliced into long strands
- Salt and pepper to taste
- ¼ cup olive oil
- 4 cloves garlic, crushed and minced
- 1 avocado, cubed
- 1 cup basil leaves
- 2 tbsp. lemon juice
- ¼ cup pistachios (unsalted)
- Cooking spray
- 1 lb. shrimp, peeled and deveined
- 2 tsp. Old Bay seasoning

Method:

1. Add the zucchini noodles in a strainer and season with salt.
2. Let sit for 30 minutes and then drain excess water.
3. In a bowl, combine the olive oil, garlic, avocado, basil leaves, lemon juice and pistachios.
4. Season with salt and pepper.
5. Transfer mixture to your food processor.
6. Pulse until smooth.
7. Spray your pan with oil.
8. Add the shrimp and season with Old Bay.
9. Cook for 3 to 5 minutes.

10. Toss the zucchini noodles in the avocado pesto and top with shrimp.

Nutritional Value:

- Calories 446
- Total Fat 33 g
- Saturated Fat 5 g
- Cholesterol 159 mg
- Sodium 713 mg
- Total Carbohydrate 16 g
- Dietary Fiber 7 g
- Protein 26 g
- Total Sugars 7 g
- Potassium 1271 mg

Baked Halibut with Brussels Sprouts

Preparation Time: 20 minutes
Cooking Time: 35 minutes
Servings: 4

Ingredients:

- 4 halibut fillets
- Salt and pepper to taste
- 4 cloves garlic, minced
- 3 tbsp. lemon juice
- 2 tbsp. melted butter
- 4 cups Brussels sprouts
- 1 tbsp. olive oil
- ¼ cup sun-dried tomatoes
- ¼ cup Kalamata olives, pitted and sliced

Method:

1. Preheat your oven to 400 degrees F.
2. Season the fish fillets with salt and pepper.
3. Top with the garlic and drizzle with a mixture of lemon and butter.
4. Bake in the oven for 20 minutes.
5. In another baking pan, toss the Brussels sprouts with oil.
6. Season with salt and pepper.
7. Bake for 15 minutes.
8. Serve the fish with the Brussels sprouts on the side, topped with sun-dried tomatoes and olives.

Nutritional Value:

- Calories 406
- Total Fat 17 g
- Saturated Fat 5 g

- Cholesterol 71 mg
- Sodium 560 mg
- Total Carbohydrate 36 g
- Dietary Fiber 8 g
- Protein 30 g
- Total Sugars 5 g
- Potassium 1379 mg

Sweet Potato Hash with Kale

Preparation Time: 15 minutes
Cooking Time: 30 minutes
Servings: 4

Ingredients:

- 1 lb. sweet potatoes, cubed
- 1 onion, sliced
- 2 tbsp. vegetable oil
- Salt and pepper to taste
- 1 tsp. garlic powder
- 4 cups kale, chopped
- 4 eggs, poached

Method:

1. Preheat your oven to 425 degrees F.
2. Toss the onion and sweet potatoes in half of the oil, salt and garlic powder.
3. Transfer to a baking pan and bake for 20 minutes.
4. Toss the kale in the remaining oil, salt and pepper.
5. Add the kale on top of the sweet potatoes and bake for another 10 minutes.
6. Serve the sweet potatoes and kale with the poached eggs on top.

Nutritional Value:

- Calories 217
- Total Fat 12 g
- Saturated Fat 2 g
- Cholesterol 186 mg
- Sodium 394 mg
- Total Carbohydrate 19 g
- Dietary Fiber 3 g
- Protein 9 g
- Total Sugars 6 g
- Potassium 525 mg

Broccoli Pasta with Turkey

Preparation Time: 15 minutes
Cooking Time: 15 minutes
Servings: 4

Ingredients:

- 6 oz. whole-wheat pasta
- 3 cups broccoli florets
- 2 cups turkey, cooked and shredded
- 1 cup cherry tomatoes, sliced in half
- ¾ cup pesto
- 1 tbsp. lemon juice
- Salt and pepper to taste
- ¼ cup Parmesan cheese, grated

Method:

1. Cook pasta according to package directions.
2. Steam the broccoli for 3 minutes.
3. Drain the pasta and broccoli.
4. Combine the rest of the ingredients in a bowl.
5. Stir in the pasta and top with the broccoli.

Nutritional Value:

- Calories 418
- Total Fat 18 g
- Saturated Fat 6 g
- Cholesterol 96 mg
- Sodium 655 mg
- Total Carbohydrate 37 g
- Dietary Fiber 6 g
- Protein 30 g
- Total Sugars 8 g
- Potassium 897 mg

Korean Beef & Cabbage

Preparation Time: 30 minutes

Cooking Time: 7 hours and 20 minutes

Servings: 8

Ingredients:

- 1 tbsp. vegetable oil
- 1 beef chuck roast, fat trimmed
- 3 tbsp. soy sauce
- ¼ cup dry white wine
- 3 tbsp. brown sugar
- 1 onion, sliced in half
- 2 tbsp. garlic, minced
- 1 jalapeño chili, chopped
- 4 cups chicken broth
- 4 cups napa cabbage, chopped
- ¾ cup Kimchi
- ¼ cup scallions, sliced thinly
- Salt and pepper to taste

Method:

1. Pour the oil into a pan over medium heat.
2. Cook the beef for 10 minutes.
3. Transfer to a slow cooker.
4. Pour the soy sauce, wine and sugar into the pan.
5. Bring to a boil.
6. Pour mixture into the slow cooker.
7. Add the rest of the ingredients except the cabbage, Kimchi, scallions, salt and pepper.
8. Cover the pot.
9. Cook on low for 7 hours.

10. Stir in the remaining ingredients and serve.

Nutritional Value:

- Calories 225
- Total Fat 7 g
- Saturated Fat 2 g
- Cholesterol 10 mg
- Sodium 634 mg
- Total Carbohydrate 11 g
- Dietary Fiber 1 g
- Protein 28 g
- Total Sugars 7 g
- Potassium 810 mg

Green Beans with Bacon

Preparation Time: 10 minutes
Cooking Time: 20 minutes
Servings: 8

Ingredients:

- 2 slices bacon, chopped
- 1 shallot, chopped
- 24 oz. green beans
- Salt and pepper to taste
- ½ tsp. smoked paprika
- 2 tsp. red wine vinegar
- 1 tsp. lemon juice

Method:

1. Preheat your oven to 450 degrees F.
2. Roast the bacon for 5 minutes.
3. Add the shallot and beans.
4. Season with salt, pepper and paprika.
5. Mix well.
6. Roast for 10 minutes.
7. Stir in the lemon juice and vinegar.
8. Roast for another 2 minutes.

Nutritional Value:

- Calories 49
- Total Fat 1 g
- Saturated Fat 0 g
- Cholesterol 3 mg
- Sodium 192 mg
- Total Carbohydrate 8 g

- Dietary Fiber 3 g
- Protein 3 g
- Total Sugars 4 g
- Potassium 249 mg

Veggie Marinara

Preparation Time: 20 minutes

Cooking Time: 5 hours and 30 minutes

Servings: 6

Ingredients:

- 1 tbsp. olive oil
- 1 cup onion, chopped
- ½ cup celery, diced
- 1 cup tomato sauce
- 6 oz. tomato paste
- 26 oz. diced tomatoes
- ½ cup dry red wine
- 8 oz. mushrooms, sliced
- 4 cloves garlic, minced
- 1 zucchini, sliced
- Salt to taste
- 1 tbsp. oregano, chopped
- 12 oz. linguine, cooked
- ¾ cup Parmesan cheese, grated
- ½ cup basil leaves

Method:

1. Pour the oil into a pan over medium heat.
2. Add the onion and celery.
3. Cook for 6 minutes.
4. Transfer to a slow cooker.
5. Stir in the rest of the ingredients except the pasta, cheese and basil.
6. Cover the pot and cook on low for 5 hours and 30 minutes.
7. Pour the marinara sauce over the noodles and sprinkle with the cheese and basil.

Nutritional Value:

- Calories 360
- Total Fat 7 g
- Saturated Fat 2 g
- Cholesterol 107 mg
- Sodium 543 mg
- Total Carbohydrate 64 g
- Dietary Fiber 11 g
- Protein 16 g
- Total Sugars 14 g
- Potassium 557 mg

Chickpea Dumplings

Preparation Time: 30 minutes
Cooking Time: 30 minutes
Servings: 4

Ingredients:

- 1 cup chickpea flour
- ¼ cup onion, chopped
- ¼ cup vegetable oil
- ¼ cup yogurt
- 4 cups spinach
- ¼ cup jalapeño pepper, chopped
- Salt to taste
- 1 tsp. mustard seeds
- 1 tsp. cumin seeds
- 2 tsp. coriander seeds
- 1 tbsp. fresh ginger, minced
- 1 tbsp. curry powder
- 15 oz. diced tomatoes
- 15 oz. tomato sauce

Method:

1. Combine the flour, onion, yogurt, spinach, jalapeño pepper and salt in a bowl.
2. Shape into dumplings.
3. Heat the oil in a pan.
4. Add the three seeds.
5. Cover and cook for 30 seconds.
6. Stir in the ginger and curry powder.
7. Add the tomatoes and tomato sauce.
8. Simmer.
9. Add the dumplings to the sauce and cook for 20 minutes.

Nutritional Value:

- Calories 454
- Total Fat 29 g
- Saturated Fat 2 g
- Cholesterol 2 mg
- Sodium 438 mg
- Total Carbohydrate 41 g
- Dietary Fiber 13 g
- Protein 12 g
- Total Sugars 13 g
- Potassium 805 mg

Tofu with Collard Greens

Preparation Time: 15 minutes

Cooking Time: 20 minutes

Servings: 4

Ingredients:

- 6 tbsp. vegetable oil, divided
- ½ cup water
- 1 lb. collards, chopped
- ½ tsp. smoked paprika
- Salt to taste
- 1 tbsp. cider vinegar
- 16 oz. tofu
- ½ tsp. onion powder
- ½ tsp. garlic powder
- 1 cup buttermilk
- 1 cup whole-wheat panko

Method:

1. Pour 1 tablespoon oil into a pot over medium low heat.
2. Pour in the water and add the collards.
3. Add the paprika, salt and vinegar.
4. Cook for 8 minutes.
5. Transfer to a plate.
6. In a dish, mix the onion powder, garlic powder and milk.
7. Coat tofu evenly with this mixture.
8. Let sit for 5 minutes.
9. Cover tofu with the breadcrumbs.
10. Add remaining oil to a pan over medium heat.
11. Cook the tofu until golden and crispy.
12. Serve with the collards.

Nutritional Value:

- Calories 366
- Total Fat 27 g
- Saturated Fat 3 g
- Cholesterol 1 mg
- Sodium 518 mg
- Total Carbohydrate 20 g
- Dietary Fiber 7 g
- Protein 17 g
- Total Sugars 2 g
- Potassium 414 mg

Eggplant Curry

Preparation Time: 20 minutes

Cooking Time: 40 minutes

Servings: 6

Ingredients:

- 2 eggplants, cubed
- Salt and pepper to taste
- 3 tbsp. olive oil, divided
- 2 cups onion, chopped
- 1 ginger, grated
- 1 tsp. garlic, grated
- 1 tbsp. red curry paste
- 2 cups tomatoes, chopped
- 15 oz. chickpeas, rinsed and drained
- 15 oz. coconut milk
- 4 cups brown rice, cooked

Method:

1. Preheat your oven to 450 degrees F.
2. Line your baking pan with foil.
3. Toss the eggplant in salt, pepper and half of the oil.
4. Bake for 20 minutes.
5. Pour the remaining oil into a pan over medium heat.
6. Cook the onion for 3 minutes.
7. Stir in the ginger, garlic and curry paste.
8. Cook for 30 seconds.
9. Add the remaining ingredients and bring to a boil.
10. Simmer for 15 minutes.
11. Add eggplant to the mixture.
12. Serve with brown rice.

Nutritional Value:

- Calories 399
- Total Fat 12 g
- Saturated Fat 4 g
- Cholesterol 10 mg
- Sodium 569 mg
- Total Carbohydrate 64 g
- Dietary Fiber 10 g
- Protein 11 g
- Total Sugars 9 g
- Potassium 770 mg

Wine-Roasted Mushrooms

Preparation Time: 5 minutes

Cooking Time: 20 minutes

Servings: 4

Ingredients:

- 1 lb. mushrooms, sliced
- 2 cups shallots, sliced
- 2 tbsp. olive oil
- Salt and pepper to taste
- 1 tbsp. thyme, chopped
- ¼ cup red wine

Method:

1. Preheat your oven to 450 degrees F.
2. Toss the mushrooms and shallots in oil.
3. Season with salt, pepper and thyme.
4. Roast for 15 minutes.
5. Stir in the wine and roast for another 5 minutes.

Nutritional Value:

- Calories 178
- Total Fat 7 g
- Saturated Fat 1 g
- Cholesterol 0 mg
- Sodium 163 mg
- Total Carbohydrate 21 g
- Dietary Fiber 4 g
- Protein 5 g
- Total Sugars 10 g
- Potassium 720 mg

Sweet & Sour Tofu with Peas

Preparation Time: 10 minutes
Cooking Time: 10 minutes
Servings: 4

Ingredients:

- ½ cup ketchup
- ¼ cup pineapple juice
- 1 tbsp. soy sauce
- 14 oz. tofu, sliced into cubes
- 1 tbsp. cornstarch
- 2 tbsp. vegetable oil
- 1 tbsp. fresh ginger, minced
- 8 oz. snow peas
- 2 tbsp. scallions, sliced thinly

Method:

1. Mix the ketchup, pineapple juice and soy sauce in a bowl. Set aside.
2. Coat all sides of tofu with cornstarch.
3. Pour the oil into a pan over medium heat.
4. Add the tofu cubes.
5. Sprinkle with ginger.
6. Cook until golden.
7. Add the peas and scallions.
8. Cook for 1 minute, stirring frequently.
9. Stir in the sauce and heat for 1 minute.

Nutritional Value:

- Calories 225
- Total Fat 11 g
- Saturated Fat 2 g

- Cholesterol 0 mg
- Sodium 504 mg
- Total Carbohydrate 23 g
- Dietary Fiber 3 g
- Protein 11 g
- Total Sugars 15 g
- Potassium 440 mg

Zucchini Fritters

Preparation Time: 30 minutes

Cooking Time: 10 minutes

Servings: 6

Ingredients:

- 2 tbsp. sour cream
- 1 tbsp. sherry vinegar
- 2 tbsp. fresh dill, chopped
- ¼ cup Greek yogurt
- 1 tbsp. water
- ½ tsp. lemon zest, grated
- 1½ lb. zucchini, grated
- Salt and pepper to taste
- 1 egg, beaten
- ¼ cup all-purpose flour
- ¼ cup cornmeal
- 2 tbsp. extra-virgin olive oil

Method:

1. In a bowl, mix the sour cream, vinegar, dill, yogurt, water, lemon zest, salt and pepper. Set aside.
2. Add the zucchini to a strainer.
3. Toss with salt. Let sit for 15 minutes.
4. Put the zucchini in a large bowl and stir in the flour, egg, cornmeal, salt and pepper.
5. Pour the oil into a pan over medium heat.
6. Drop a small amount of the batter into the pan.
7. Cook for 2 minutes per side.
8. Repeat with the remaining batter.
9. Serve with the sauce.

Nutritional Value:

- Calories 105
- Total Fat 6 g
- Saturated Fat 1 g
- Cholesterol 26 mg
- Sodium 292 mg
- Total Carbohydrate 10 g
- Dietary Fiber 1 g
- Protein 4 g
- Total Sugars 2 g
- Potassium 270 mg

Roasted Veggies

Preparation Time: 20 minutes
Cooking Time: 25 minutes
Servings: 5

Ingredients:

- 1 cup broccoli florets
- 2 cups cauliflower florets
- 2 cloves garlic, sliced thinly
- 1 tbsp. olive oil
- Salt to taste
- 1 tsp. dried oregano, crushed
- ¾ cup red bell pepper, diced
- ¾ cup zucchini, diced
- 2 tsp. lemon zest

Method:

1. Preheat your oven to 425 degrees F.
2. Mix the broccoli, cauliflower and garlic in a baking pan.
3. Toss in oil and season with salt and oregano.
4. Roast in the oven for 10 minutes.
5. Stir in the zucchini and bell pepper.
6. Roast for 15 minutes.
7. Sprinkle the lemon zest on top of the veggies.

Nutritional Value:

- Calories 52
- Total Fat 3 g
- Saturated Fat 0 g
- Cholesterol 0mg
- Sodium 134 mg

- Total Carbohydrate 5 g
- Dietary Fiber 2 g
- Protein 2 g
- Total Sugars 2 g
- Potassium 270 mg

Tofu & Mushroom Stir-Fry

Preparation Time: 15 minutes

Cooking Time: 11 minutes

Servings: 5

Ingredients:

- 4 tbsp. peanut oil, divided
- 1 red bell pepper, diced
- 1 lb. mushrooms, sliced
- 1 clove garlic, grated
- 1 tbsp. ginger, grated
- 1 cup scallions, sliced
- 8 oz. baked tofu, diced
- 3 tbsp. oyster sauce

Method:

1. Pour half of the oil into a pan over medium heat.
2. Add the bell pepper and mushrooms.
3. Cook for 4 minutes.
4. Add the garlic, scallions and ginger.
5. Cook for 30 seconds, stirring frequently.
6. Transfer veggie mixture to a bowl.
7. Pour the remaining oil into the pan.
8. Cook the tofu for 5 minutes.
9. Stir in the veggies and oyster sauce.
10. Cook for 1 minute.

Nutritional Value:

- Calories 171
- Total Fat 13 g
- Saturated Fat 2 g

- Cholesterol 0 mg
- Sodium 309 mg
- Total Carbohydrate 9 g
- Dietary Fiber 2 g
- Protein 8 g
- Total Sugars 3 g
- Potassium 469 mg

Potato & Artichoke Gratin

Preparation Time: 30 minutes

Cooking Time: 1 hour and 40 minutes

Servings: 16

Ingredients:

- 1 tbsp. olive oil
- 1 leek, sliced
- 2 cups heavy cream
- 1 cup milk, divided
- Salt and pepper to taste
- 1 tbsp. cornstarch
- 2 cups Parmesan cheese, grated and divided
- 14 oz. artichokes, rinsed, drained and chopped
- 2 lb. potatoes, sliced thickly
- 2 tbsp. capers, rinsed and patted dry

Method:

1. Preheat your oven to 325 degrees F.
2. Pour the oil into a pan over medium heat.
3. Cook the leeks for 3 minutes.
4. Transfer to another plate.
5. Mix the cream, half of the milk and salt in a saucepan over medium heat.
6. Cook for 2 minutes.
7. Mix the remaining milk and cornstarch in a bowl.
8. Add this to the cream mixture and cook for 3 minutes.
9. Remove from the stove.
10. Stir in the Parmesan cheese.
11. Arrange the artichokes and potatoes in a baking pan.
12. Season with salt and pepper.
13. Pour the cream mixture on top.

14. Sprinkle the leeks and capers on top.
15. Bake in the oven for 1 hour and 25 minutes.

Nutritional Value:

- Calories 209
- Total Fat 12 g
- Saturated Fat 7 g
- Cholesterol 34 mg
- Sodium 286 mg
- Total Carbohydrate 19 g
- Dietary Fiber 2 g
- Protein 7 g
- Total Sugars 3 g
- Potassium 423 mg

Grilled Zucchini with Tomato Salsa

Preparation Time: 10 minutes

Cooking Time: 8 minutes

Servings: 4

Ingredients:

- 4 zucchinis, sliced
- 1 tbsp. olive oil
- Salt and pepper to taste
- 1 cup tomatoes, chopped
- 1 tbsp. mint, chopped
- 1 tsp. red wine vinegar

Method:

1. Preheat your grill.
2. Coat the zucchini with oil and season with salt and pepper.
3. Grill for 4 minutes per side.
4. Mix the remaining ingredients in a bowl.
5. Top the grilled zucchini with the minty salsa.

Nutritional Value:

- Calories 71
- Total Fat 5 g
- Saturated Fat 1 g
- Cholesterol 0 mg
- Sodium 157 mg
- Total Carbohydrate 6 g
- Dietary Fiber 2 g
- Protein 2 g
- Total Sugars 4 g
- Potassium 413 mg

Eggplant Parmesan

Preparation Time: 20 minutes

Cooking Time: 1 hour

Servings: 8

Ingredients:

- Cooking spray
- 2 eggplants, sliced into rounds
- Salt and pepper to taste
- 2 tbsp. olive oil
- 1 cup onion, chopped
- 2 cloves garlic, crushed and minced
- 28 oz. crushed tomatoes
- ¼ cup red wine
- 1 tsp. dried basil
- 1 tsp. dried oregano
- ½ cup Parmesan cheese
- 1 cup mozzarella cheese
- Basil leaves, chopped

Method:

1. Preheat your oven to 400 degrees F.
2. Spray your baking pan with oil.
3. Arrange the eggplant in the baking pan.
4. Season with salt and pepper.
5. Roast for 20 minutes.
6. In a pan over medium heat, add the oil and cook the onion for 4 minutes.
7. Add the garlic and cook for 1 to 2 minutes.
8. Stir in the rest of the ingredients except the cheese and basil.
9. Simmer for 10 minutes.
10. Spread the sauce on a baking dish.

11. Top with the eggplant slices.
12. Sprinkle the mozzarella and Parmesan on top.
13. Bake in the oven for 25 minutes.

Nutritional Value:

- Calories 192
- Total Fat 9 g
- Saturated Fat 4 g
- Cholesterol 18 mg
- Sodium 453 mg
- Total Carbohydrate 16 g
- Dietary Fiber 5 g
- Protein 10 g
- Total Sugars 8 g
- Potassium 632 mg

Chapter 6: Snack and Sides

Green Pizza with Bacon

Preparation Time: 10 minutes
Cooking Time: 16 minutes
Servings: 4

Ingredients:

- 1 whole-wheat pizza crust
- ½ cup pizza sauce
- 2 oz. mozzarella cheese
- ½ cup kale, chopped
- 4 slices bacon, cooked and sliced
- ¼ cup pineapple slices

Method:

1. Preheat your oven to 450 degrees F.
2. Put the pizza crust on a baking pan and bake for 7 to 8 minutes.
3. Take it out of the oven and spread pizza sauce on top.
4. Sprinkle with the cheese, kale, bacon and pineapple slices.
5. Bake in the oven for another 8 minutes.

Nutritional Value:

- Calories 276
- Total Fat 8 g
- Saturated Fat 4 g
- Cholesterol 12 mg
- Sodium 551 mg
- Total Carbohydrate 40 g
- Dietary Fiber 7 g
- Protein 14 g
- Total Sugars 7 g
- Potassium 175 mg

Roasted Vegetables & Sausage Sandwich

Preparation Time: 15 minutes

Cooking Time: 3 hours and 10 minutes

Servings: 4

Ingredients:

- 2 tsp. olive oil, divided
- 2 turkey or chicken sausage links
- 1 onion, sliced
- 4 cloves garlic, crushed and minced
- 1 red bell pepper, sliced
- 1 cup cherry tomatoes
- 1 tsp. dried oregano, crushed
- 2 tsp. honey mustard
- 3 tbsp. mayonnaise
- 4 hot dog buns, toasted

Method:

1. Spray your slow cooker with oil.
2. Pour half of the olive oil into a pan over medium heat.
3. Cook the sausage until brown.
4. Transfer to the slow cooker.
5. Pour the remaining oil, onion, garlic, bell pepper and tomatoes into the slow cooker.
6. Season with oregano.
7. Cover the pot.
8. Cook on high for 3 hours.
9. Combine the mustard and mayo in a bowl.
10. Spread this mixture on the hotdog buns.
11. Stuff each with the sausage and vegetables.

Nutritional Value:

- Calories 308
- Total Fat 12 g
- Saturated Fat 3 g
- Cholesterol 34 mg
- Sodium 596 mg
- Total Carbohydrate 36 g
- Dietary Fiber 3 g
- Protein 13 g
- Total Sugars 11 g
- Potassium 222 mg

Avocado Salad in a Sandwich

Preparation Time: 10 minutes
Cooking Time: 0 minute
Servings: 2

Ingredients:

- 4 whole-wheat bread slices
- ¼ cup hummus
- Pepper to taste
- 1 cup arugula leaves
- ½ avocado, sliced
- ½ cup Gruyere cheese, grated

Method:

1. Spread each bread slice with hummus and sprinkle with pepper.
2. Arrange the arugula and avocado on top of the bread slices.
3. Sprinkle with the Gruyere.
4. Top with another slice.
5. Toast until the cheese has melted.

Nutritional Value:

- Calories 235
- Total Fat 12 g
- Saturated Fat 3 g
- Cholesterol 16 mg
- Sodium 354 mg
- Total Carbohydrate 26 g
- Dietary Fiber 8 g
- Protein 11 g
- Total Sugars 3 g
- Potassium 116 mg

Vegetable Wraps

Preparation Time: 10 minutes
Cooking Time: 0 minute
Servings: 4

Ingredients:

- 4 tortilla wraps
- 1 cup hummus
- 1 cup baby spinach
- 2 oz. cheddar cheese slices
- 1 cup red bell pepper, sliced
- 1 cup broccoli florets, chopped
- 1 cup carrots, julienned
- 1 cup red cabbage, shredded

Method:

1. Spread the tortilla with hummus.
2. Top with the spinach, cheddar, red bell pepper, broccoli, carrots and cabbage, and roll.

Nutritional Value:

- Calories 391
- Total Fat 19 g
- Saturated Fat 5 g
- Cholesterol 14 mg
- Sodium 791 mg
- Total Carbohydrate 40 g
- Dietary Fiber 7 g
- Protein 13 g
- Total Sugars 6 g
- Potassium 214 mg

Turkey Sandwich

Preparation Time: 15 minutes
Cooking Time: 15 minutes
Servings: 2

Ingredients:

- 1 tsp. Dijon mustard
- 1 tbsp. mayonnaise
- ½ tsp. maple syrup
- 1 tsp. parsley, chopped
- 1 tsp. dill, chopped
- 2 whole-wheat bread slices, toasted
- 1 tbsp. cold turkey gravy
- ½ cup lettuce, shredded
- ¼ avocado, sliced
- 3 oz. turkey breast fillet, cooked and sliced thinly
- 1 slice Gouda cheese
- 2 strips bacon, sliced
- 1 tsp. olive oil
- 1 tsp. white vinegar
- Pepper to taste
- 1 tbsp. cranberry sauce

Method:

1. Mix the mustard, mayo, maple syrup, parsley and dill in a bowl.
2. Spread one bread slice with this mixture.
3. Top it with gravy.
4. Arrange the lettuce, avocado, turkey and cheese on top.
5. Drizzle with the oil, vinegar and season with pepper.
6. Spread the cranberry sauce on top of the other bread slice and place this on top of the sandwich.

Nutritional Value:

- Calories 340
- Total Fat 19 g
- Saturated Fat 5 g
- Cholesterol 54 mg
- Sodium 464 mg
- Total Carbohydrate 21 g
- Dietary Fiber 4 g
- Protein 22 g
- Total Sugars 7 g
- Potassium 397 mg

Garlic Mashed Potatoes

Preparation Time: 20 minutes
Cooking Time: 10 minutes
Servings: 4

Ingredients:

- 2 lb. potatoes, sliced into cubes
- 6 cloves garlic
- Salt and pepper to taste
- ½ cup chicken broth
- 2 tbsp. sour cream
- Pinch nutmeg

Method:

1. Add the garlic and potatoes in a pot with water.
2. Season with salt.
3. Cover the pot.
4. Boil until potatoes are tender.
5. Drain the potatoes and mash with fork or potato masher.
6. Stir in broth and add the sour cream.
7. Season with nutmeg, salt and pepper.

Nutritional Value:

- Calories 135
- Total Fat 1 g
- Saturated Fat 0 g
- Cholesterol 2 mg
- Sodium 446 mg
- Total Carbohydrate 30 g
- Dietary Fiber 3 g
- Protein 3 g
- Total Sugars 1 g
- Potassium 502 mg

Green Beans with Roasted Red Peppers

Preparation Time: 10 minutes
Cooking Time: 12 minutes
Servings: 6

Ingredients:

- 1 tbsp. olive oil
- 1 cup onion, chopped
- 1 tbsp. balsamic vinegar
- ½ cup roasted red peppers, chopped
- ¼ cup olives, pitted and sliced
- 2 tbsp. fresh basil, chopped
- Salt and pepper to taste
- 1 lb. green beans, sliced and steamed

Method:

1. Pour the oil into a pan over medium heat.
2. Cook the onion for 10 minutes.
3. Pour in the vinegar and cook for 2 minutes, stirring frequently.
4. Add the olives, red peppers, salt, pepper and basil.
5. Cook for 2 minutes and remove from heat.
6. Combine the red pepper mixture and green beans.

Nutritional Value:

- Calories 73
- Total Fat 3 g
- Saturated Fat 0 g
- Cholesterol 0 mg
- Sodium 153 mg
- Total Carbohydrate 11 g
- Dietary Fiber 4 g
- Protein 2 g
- Total Sugars 3 g
- Potassium 248 mg

Zucchini Fries & Dip

Preparation Time: 20 minutes

Cooking Time: 30 minutes

Servings: 6

Ingredients:

- Cooking spray
- 1 zucchini, sliced into strips
- 2 eggs
- 1 tbsp. water
- ¾ whole-wheat breadcrumbs
- 2 tsp. Old Bay seasoning
- Pepper to taste
- 1 tbsp. lemon juice
- 2 tbsp. mayonnaise
- ¼ cup Greek yogurt
- ½ tsp. garlic powder
- Salt to taste
- 1/8 cup chives, chopped
- 1/8 cup parsley, chopped

Method:

1. Preheat your oven to 425 degrees F.
2. Spray a baking pan with oil.
3. Mix the eggs and water in a bowl.
4. Add the breadcrumbs, Old Bay seasoning and pepper in another bowl.
5. Dip the zucchini strips in the first and second bowls.
6. Arrange on the baking pan.
7. Bake for 30 minutes.
8. Mix the rest of the ingredients in a dipping bowl.
9. Serve the fries with the dip.

Nutritional Value:

- Calories 84
- Total Fat 5 g
- Saturated Fat 1 g
- Cholesterol 30 mg
- Sodium 237 mg
- Total Carbohydrate 7 g
- Dietary Fiber 1 g
- Protein 4 g
- Total Sugars 2 g
- Potassium 182 mg

Roasted Mushrooms

Preparation Time: 15 minutes
Cooking Time: 20 minutes
Servings: 6

Ingredients:

- 1 lb. fresh mushrooms, sliced
- 6 cloves garlic, sliced
- 2 tbsp. olive oil
- 2 tsp. balsamic vinegar
- 2 tsp. Worcestershire sauce
- 1 tsp. dried oregano
- Salt and pepper to taste
- 2 tbsp. parsley, chopped

Method:

1. Preheat your oven to 400°F.
2. Add the mushrooms on a baking pan.
3. Stir in the garlic.
4. Drizzle the top with oil, vinegar, and Worcestershire sauce.
5. Season with salt, pepper and oregano.
6. Roast for 20 minutes.
7. Sprinkle with parsley before serving.

Nutritional Value:

- Calories 65
- Total Fat 5 g
- Saturated Fat 1 g
- Cholesterol 0 mg
- Sodium 124 mg
- Total Carbohydrate 4 g

- Dietary Fiber 1 g
- Protein 5 g
- Total Sugars 2 g
- Potassium 650 mg

Roasted Brussels Sprouts

Preparation Time: 10 minutes

Cooking Time: 15 minutes

Servings: 4

Ingredients:

- Cooking spray
- 1 lb. Brussels sprouts, sliced in half
- 1 tsp. olive oil
- Salt and pepper to taste
- 1 tbsp. lemon juice

Method:

1. Preheat your oven to 425 degrees F.
2. Line your baking sheet with foil.
3. Spray with oil.
4. Toss the Brussels sprouts in oil and season with salt and pepper.
5. Roast for 15 minutes.
6. Drizzle with lemon juice before serving.

Nutritional Value:

- Calories 65
- Total Fat 2 g
- Saturated Fat 0 g
- Cholesterol 0 mg
- Sodium 152 mg
- Total Carbohydrate 11 g
- Dietary Fiber 4 g
- Protein 4 g
- Total Sugars 3 g
- Potassium 398 mg

Chapter 7: Desserts

Sweetened Pears

Preparation Time: 10 minutes

Cooking Time: 50 minutes

Servings: 4

Ingredients:

- 4 pears, peeled
- ¼ cup sugar
- 12 oz. dry white wine
- 1 cinnamon stick
- 2 tsp. orange zest
- 1 ½ cups water
- ½ cup yogurt
- 1 pod vanilla bean, split

Method:

1. Use a melon baller to scoop balls from the melons.
2. Transfer to a bowl and set aside.
3. In a pan over medium high heat, mix the sugar, wine, cinnamon stick, orange zest and water.
4. Bring to a boil and simmer until the sugar has dissolved.
5. Toss the pears in the wine mixture.
6. Cook for 30 minutes.
7. Transfer the pears in a bowl.
8. Cook the syrup for 10 minutes.
9. Pour the syrup over the pears and serve with yogurt mixed with vanilla.

Nutritional Value:

- Calories 276

- Total Fat 1 g
- Saturated Fat 1 g
- Cholesterol 5 mg
- Sodium 18 mg
- Total Carbohydrate 51 g
- Dietary Fiber 7 g
- Protein 3 g
- Total Sugars 37 g
- Potassium 263 mg

Roasted Plums

Preparation Time: 10 minutes
Cooking Time: 20 minutes
Servings: 6

Ingredients:

- Cooking spray
- 6 plums, pitted and sliced in half
- ½ cup pineapple juice
- ½ tsp. ground cinnamon
- 3 tbsp. brown sugar, divided
- ⅛ tsp. ground cumin
- ¼ tsp. ground cardamom
- ¼ cup sour cream
- 2 tbsp. almonds, toasted and slivered

Method:

1. Spray your baking pan with oil.
2. Add the plums in the baking pan.
3. Mix with the pineapple juice, cinnamon, 2 tablespoons sugar, cumin and cardamom.
4. Pour the mixture over the plums.
5. Bake in the oven for 450 degrees F for 20 minutes.
6. In a bowl, mix the sour cream and remaining sugar.
7. Arrange the roasted plums in a serving bowl.
8. Top with the sweetened sour cream and almonds.

Nutritional Value:

- Calories 102
- Total Fat 3 g

- Saturated Fat 1 g
- Cholesterol 4 mg
- Sodium 12 mg
- Total Carbohydrate 19 g
- Dietary Fiber 1 g
- Protein 2 g
- Total Sugars 17 g
- Potassium 209 mg

Sweetened Mango & Coconut Flakes

Preparation Time: 10 minutes
Cooking Time: 10 minutes
Servings: 4

Ingredients:

- 2 mangoes, sliced into cubes
- 2 tsp. crystallized ginger, chopped
- 2 tsp. orange zest
- 2 tbsp. coconut flakes

Method:

1. Preheat your oven to 350 degrees F.
2. Add the mangoes to muffin pan.
3. In a bowl, mix the remaining ingredients and pour over the mangoes.
4. Roast in the oven for 10 minutes.

Nutritional Value:

- Calories 89
- Total Fat 2 g
- Saturated Fat 1 g
- Cholesterol 0 mg
- Sodium 14 mg
- Total Carbohydrate 20 g
- Dietary Fiber 2 g
- Protein 1 g
- Total Sugars 17 g
- Potassium 177 mg

Fruit Compote

Preparation Time: 10 minutes
Cooking Time: 8 minutes
Servings: 10

Ingredients:

- 3 tbsp. orange juice
- 15 oz. pineapple chunks
- ¾ cup dried apricots, sliced into quarters
- 3 pears, sliced into cubes
- 1 tsp. ginger, grated
- 1 tbsp. tapioca
- 2 cups cherries, pitted and sliced
- ¼ cup coconut flakes, toasted

Method:

1. Pour the orange juice into a slow cooker.
2. Stir in the pineapple, apricots, pears, ginger and tapioca.
3. Cover the pot and cook for 8 hours on low setting.
4. Stir in the cherries.
5. Sprinkle coconut flakes on top before serving.

Nutritional Value:

- Calories 124
- Total Fat 1 g
- Saturated Fat 1 g
- Cholesterol 0 mg
- Sodium 10 mg
- Total Carbohydrate 29 g
- Dietary Fiber 3 g
- Protein 3 g
- Total Sugars 23 g
- Potassium 275 mg

Figs with Walnuts, Honey & Yogurt

Preparation Time: 5 minutes

Cooking Time: 0 minute

Servings: 4

Ingredients:

- 2 figs, sliced
- 2 tsp. honey
- ½ tsp. vanilla
- 8 oz. yogurt, refrigerated for 8 hours
- 1 tbsp. walnuts, chopped and toasted

Method:

1. Combine all the ingredients except walnuts in a serving bowl.
2. Sprinkle the walnuts on top.

Nutritional Value:

- Calories 157
- Total Fat 4 g
- Saturated Fat 1 g
- Cholesterol 7 mg
- Sodium 80 mg
- Total Carbohydrate 24 g
- Dietary Fiber 2 g
- Protein 7 g
- Total Sugars 4 g
- Potassium 550 mg

Berries & Orange Cream

Preparation Time: 3 hours and 10 minutes

Cooking Time: 0 minute

Servings: 12

Ingredients:

- 1 tbsp. honey
- 3 tbsp. freshly squeezed orange juice
- 1 tsp. balsamic vinegar
- 2 cups blueberries, sliced
- 2 cups blackberries, sliced
- 1 cup raspberries, sliced
- 1 cup strawberries, sliced
- ½ cup light sour cream
- 1 tsp. orange zest

Method:

1. Pour the honey, orange juice and vinegar in a glass jar with lid.
2. Shake to mix well.
3. Place all the berries in a bowl.
4. Pour the mixture over the berries and coat evenly.
5. Cover with foil and refrigerate for 3 hours.
6. Combine the sour cream and orange zest.
7. Serve berries with the orange cream.

Nutritional Value:

- Calories 64
- Total Fat 2 g
- Saturated Fat 1 g
- Cholesterol 3 mg
- Sodium 7 mg

- Total Carbohydrate 12 g
- Dietary Fiber 2 g
- Protein 1 g
- Total Sugars 6 g
- Potassium 110 mg

Yogurt Strawberries

Preparation Time: 1 hour and 5 minutes
Cooking Time: 0 minute
Servings: 1

Ingredients:

- 3 strawberries, sliced
- 1 tbsp. plain Greek yogurt

Method:

1. Combine the strawberries and yogurt.
2. Refrigerate for 1 hour.

Nutritional Value:

- Calories 20
- Total Fat 4 g
- Saturated Fat 1 g
- Cholesterol 0 mg
- Sodium 1 mg
- Total Carbohydrate 8 g
- Dietary Fiber 4 g
- Protein 12 g
- Total Sugars 2 g
- Potassium 201 mg

Fruit Salad

Preparation Time: 4 hours and 15 minutes

Cooking Time: 0 minute

Servings: 6

Ingredients:

- ½ cream cheese
- 1 tbsp. honey
- 6 oz. Greek yogurt
- 1 tsp. orange zest
- 1 tsp. lemon zest
- 1 mango, sliced into cubes
- 1 orange, sliced into sections
- 3 kiwifruits, sliced
- 1 cup blueberries

Method:

1. In a bowl, beat the cream cheese using an electric mixer.
2. Mix until smooth.
3. Stir in the honey and yogurt.
4. Add the orange zest and lemon zest.
5. Mix well.
6. Divide the mangoes, oranges, blueberries and kiwis in serving bowls.
7. Top with the cream cheese.
8. Chill for 4 hours before serving.

Nutritional Value:

- Calories 131
- Total Fat 3 g
- Saturated Fat 2 g
- Cholesterol 9 mg

- Sodium 102 mg
- Total Carbohydrate 23 g
- Dietary Fiber 3 g
- Protein 5 g
- Total Sugars 18 g
- Potassium 234 mg

Berries with Ginger

Preparation Time: 1 hour and 10 minutes
Cooking Time: 0 minute
Servings: 2

Ingredients:

- ½ cup yogurt
- ½ cup raspberries
- ½ cup blueberries
- 2 gingersnap cookies, crushed

Method:

1. Add the yogurt into a bowl.
2. Top with the blueberries and raspberries.
3. Sprinkle the cookie powder on top.
4. Refrigerate for 10 hours before serving.

Nutritional Value:

- Calories 88
- Total Fat 1 g
- Saturated Fat 0 g
- Cholesterol 0 mg
- Sodium 62 mg
- Total Carbohydrate 14 g
- Dietary Fiber 2 g
- Protein 7 g
- Total Sugars 7 g
- Potassium 71 mg

Dessert Nachos

Preparation Time: 10 minutes
Cooking Time: 8 minutes
Servings: 6

Ingredients:

- Cooking spray
- 2 tbsp. sugar, divided
- ¼ tsp. cinnamon powder
- 3 tortillas
- ¼ cup sour cream
- ½ cup cream cheese
- ¼ cup orange juice
- 1 tsp. orange zest
- 2 cups melon, sliced into cubes

Method:

1. Preheat your oven to 425 degrees F.
2. Spray your baking pan with oil.
3. In a bowl, mix the cinnamon and half of the sugar.
4. Spray both sides of tortilla with oil.
5. Sprinkle the cinnamon mixture on both sides.
6. Slice the tortillas into wedges.
7. Add to the baking pan and bake for 4 minutes.
8. Flip the wedges and bake for another 4 minutes.
9. In a bowl, combine the rest of the ingredients except the melon cubes with the remaining sugar.
10. Spread this mixture on top of the wedges and top with the melons.

Nutritional Value:

- Calories 121

- Total Fat 5 g
- Saturated Fat 3 g
- Cholesterol 14 mg
- Sodium 207 mg
- Total Carbohydrate 18 g
- Dietary Fiber 5 g
- Protein 5 g
- Total Sugars 11 g
- Potassium 183 mg

Chapter 8: Drinks

Fruity Smoothie

Preparation Time: 10 minutes
Cooking Time: 0 minute
Servings: 1

Ingredients:

- ¾ cup plain yogurt
- ½ cup pineapple juice
- 1 cup pineapple chunks
- 1 cup raspberries, sliced
- 1 cup blueberries, sliced

Method:

1. Process the ingredients in a blender.
2. Chill before serving.

Nutritional Value:

- Calories 279
- Total Fat 2 g
- Saturated Fat 0 g
- Cholesterol 4 mg
- Sodium 149 mg
- Total Carbohydrate 56 g
- Dietary Fiber 7 g
- Protein 12 g
- Total Sugars 46 g
- Potassium 719 mg

Pineapple, Banana & Spinach Smoothie

Preparation Time: 10 minutes

Cooking Time: 0 minute

Servings: 1

Ingredients:

- ½ cup almond milk
- ¼ cup yogurt
- 1 cup spinach
- 1 cup banana
- 1 cup pineapple chunks
- 1 tbsp. chia seeds

Method:

1. Add all the ingredients in a blender.
2. Blend until smooth.
3. Chill in the refrigerator before serving.

Nutritional Value:

- Calories 297
- Total Fat 6 g
- Saturated Fat 1 g
- Cholesterol 4 mg
- Sodium 145 mg
- Total Carbohydrate 54 g
- Dietary Fiber 10 g
- Protein 13 g
- Total Sugars 29 g
- Potassium 1038 mg

Kale & Avocado Smoothie

Preparation Time: 10 minutes
Cooking Time: 0 minute
Servings: 1

Ingredients:

- 1 ripe banana
- 1 cup kale
- 1 cup almond milk
- ¼ avocado
- 1 tbsp. chia seeds
- 2 tsp. honey
- 1 cup ice cubes

Method:

1. Blend all the ingredients until smooth.

Nutritional Value:

- Calories 343
- Total Fat 14 g
- Saturated Fat 2 g
- Cholesterol 0 mg
- Sodium 199 mg
- Total Carbohydrate 55 g
- Dietary Fiber 12 g
- Protein 6 g
- Total Sugars 29 g
- Potassium 1051 mg

Vegetable & Tomato Juice

Preparation Time: 10 minutes
Cooking Time: 0 minute
Servings: 2

Ingredients:

- 1 cup Romaine lettuce
- ¼ cup fresh chives, chopped
- 2 tomatoes, sliced
- 1 red bell pepper, sliced
- 2 stalks celery, chopped
- 1 carrot, chopped

Method:

1. Process the ingredients in proper order using a juicer.
2. Pour the juice into glasses and serve.

Nutritional Value:

- Calories 46
- Total Fat 0 g
- Saturated Fat 0 g
- Cholesterol 0 mg
- Sodium 82 mg
- Total Carbohydrate 9 g
- Dietary Fiber 2 g
- Protein 1 g
- Total Sugars 7 g
- Potassium 466 mg

Orange & Carrot Juice

Preparation Time: 15 minutes
Cooking Time: 0 minute
Servings: 2

Ingredients:

- 1 tomato, sliced
- 1 orange, sliced into wedges
- 1 apple, sliced
- 4 carrots, sliced
- Ice cubes

Method:

1. Follow the order of the ingredients list when processing these through the juice.
2. Transfer the juice into glasses.
3. Fill your glass with ice and serve.

Nutritional Value:

- Calories 111
- Total Fat 1 g
- Saturated Fat 0 g
- Cholesterol 0 mg
- Sodium 38 mg
- Total Carbohydrate 24 g
- Dietary Fiber 1 g
- Protein 2 g
- Total Sugars 18 g
- Potassium 434 mg

Apple & Spinach Juice

Preparation Time: 10 minutes

Cooking Time: 0 minute

Servings: 2

Ingredients:

- 1½ cups spinach
- ½ grapefruit, sliced
- 2 apples, sliced
- 1 small ginger, sliced
- 2 stalks celery

Method:

1. Process the ingredients in your juicer following the order in the list.
2. Pour juice into glasses and chill before serving.

Nutritional Value:

- Calories 55
- Total Fat 0 g
- Saturated Fat 0 g
- Cholesterol 0 mg
- Sodium 60 mg
- Total Carbohydrate 13 g
- Dietary Fiber 1 g
- Protein 1 g
- Total Sugars 10 g
- Potassium 150 mg

Conclusion

Living a healthy lifestyle starts with a healthy diet.

If you want to protect yourself from health problems and live a longer and better-quality life, it would be a good idea to adopt a healthy and well-balanced diet.

One that will certainly do wonders for you is the plant-based diet.

It's a diet that focuses on the consumption of fruits, vegetables and other plant-derived food products.

This will help you reduce the risk of ailments such as heart disease, type 2 diabetes, high blood pressure and so on.

And the great thing about this is that you don't have to completely eliminate a food group in your diet, but just make small changes in your diet for the benefit of your physical and mental health.

Good luck!

www.ingramcontent.com/pod-product-compliance
Lightning Source LLC
LaVergne TN
LVHW082342130125
801208LV00035B/877
* 9 7 8 1 7 1 2 7 4 7 2 5 4 *